How to ADOPT A PELICAN

***

CONVERSATIONS with PELICAN
Volume 1

Cheryl M Tyler

LANDLOCKED PELICAN PUBLICATIONS
Lubbock, Texas 79414
landlockedpelican.com

Copyright 2021 by CMTI
and Landlocked Pelican Publications

ISBN Paperback
978-1-956156-11-9

Art and photography by Cheryl M Tyler
This is a work of fiction. Names, characters, places, and incidents are products of the author's imagination or are used fictitiously. Any resemblance to persons, living or dead, business establishments, events, or locales is entirely coincidental.

PRAISE FOR CONVERSATIONS WITH PELICAN

"Mama, did Pelican write this? It's good! Best book I read this year! I like the part about the Pelican of Toledo Avenue!"—*Gertrude Stein, spotty dog extraordinaire*

"I'm gonna marry Pelican someday. He's the best!"—*Suzanne, French bulldog, canine star of Two-Part Inventions*

"I wish the Pelican write a hunderrd books! Me and my peeples woold rede them all!!—*Truffle, mastiff-doxie-Yorkie*

"We're totally confused . . . what is this Pelican?! A bird? Sounds like he might be a cat or a bird . . . or a DOG?! Read the book to find out!"—*Tat the cat and Puddy the house dawg*

"I buyed five coppies for my mudder!"—*Patch, springer spaniel and obedience champion*

"Pelican okay puppy but I dowwt he can writte. I gonna bitte him."—*Jill, in charge of all doggos and pedestrians*

"I hear tell that famous lady doc is writing books with ANOTHER dog, some weirdo named Pelican, of all things! Hmph!"—*Chester the wannabe Norwich terrier*

"I gona curl up by th fireplac and reed this Pelican book! The MUST READ of the Pacifik north."—*Luckenbach, black lab and shop dog, dog star of Luckenbach North*

"*HOW TO ADOPT A PELICAN* is better than dogfood!"—*Prince Hairy, extra-hairy old English sheepdog*

"Mom, Mom! Did you know Pelican's mom is writing a book with him?"
"Yes, Attie. There are lots of great dog stories!"
"Don't tell Pelican that. He thinks he's the only dog with stories."
"I like Pelican. Do you?"
"Yes."
"Would you like me to write stories about you?"
"Absolutely not!"
"Why not?"
"I am NOT revealing MY secrets for the world to know."—A*ttie, rescued red heeler and possum chaser*

"I like *HOW TO ADOPT A PELICAN!*"—*I tink the part about me is the besty part.*"
    --*Marie Bracquemond*

"When do I get to meet this hunkhunka hairy dog, Pelican?"—*Lucy in the Sky with Diamonds*

"Yawm. Dogs are just sooooo boring. Now, if Pelican and I were to meet, I'm sure he'd have some interesting tails to tell."—*Sabrina, the Magnificent*

"Yes, but can Pelican meow? No doubt . . . negatory."—*Cat Stephens, researcher of cat vocal utterances*

"Pelican big hairy dog like me. I give his book five barks!"—*T.S. Eliot, Great Pyrenees doggo*

"Dogs no can spell! I'll bet his mama wrote it!" *Nodak, calico cat*

"Pelican should win the Pawlitzer Prize for his debut book!"—*Wentletrap, that busy little guy*

HOW TO ADOPT A PELICAN

is dedicated to
Tena Price
and
Dalmatian Rescue of Colorado.

*Thanks for getting Meadowlark, Rex Lee,
and their eight babies out of the woods
and bringing the
Pelican into our lives!*

Acknowledgements

Thank you to everyone on Team Pelican!
Much appreciation goes to **Paul Epstein,
Marsha Gillis, Keith Hagel, Helen Joffe,
John Karris,** and **Carole Miller**
for your valuable contributions to
HOW TO ADOPT A PELICAN!

Thanks to the following for providing pawsitively amazing
book reviews from your own amazing pets:
**Paul Epstein, La Nelle Ethridge,
Helen Joffe,** and **Betsy King**.

Works by Cheryl M Tyler

Please visit landlockedpelican.com for more information.

CONVERSATIONS with PELICAN

How to Adopt a Pelican
Sorry, Mama*!*
The Perplexed Pelican
Pelican of Toledo Avenue
Fluffbutt Cowboy

CONVERSATIONS with BENNIE

Life of Bennie
Bennie and the Pets
I Get by with Help from My Peoples
The Hair Snatchers*!*
Gentleman Dog about Town
Home Sweet Doghouse

Novels: COMPLICATED LIVES series

Star Mountain
Luckenbach North
Two-Part Inventions
Finding Hollister

TROUVERE: A Literary Journal

Volume 1
Cheryl M Tyler, Editor

Check out landlockedpelican.com for all the latest.
(Some titles pending publication.)

CHAPTER ONE
BABY PELICAN

PELICAN: Who are all these dogs?!

ME: Meadowlark is your mama, and these are all your brothers and sisters.

PELICAN: There are a lot of us!

ME: Yes, there are. Your mama gave birth to 8 puppies!

PELICAN: That's a lot! I like having so many puppies to play with!

ME: You're all extremely adorable!

PELICAN: I'm adorable?

ME: 'Fraid so.

PELICAN: Has my mama always lived here?

ME: That's a very good question. She and your daddy were dumped in the woods in central Texas, along with some other dogs. You puppies were probably born in the woods, and then people found you.

PELICAN: Who found me?

ME: The person who owns the woods and a lady named Tena who helps dogs who have no homes.

PELICAN: So how did we come here?

ME: Miss Tena asked for help, and I responded. Tena brought you here to your foster home. She drove over 700 miles to get you here!

PELICAN: That was very nice of her. Will you tell her thank you from me?

ME: I will. She'll be glad to know you're happy about it!

PELICAN: I send her Pelican kisses!!!

PELICAN: Mama, what happened when we got in the big box thing?

ME: The big box thing is our truck. We went to the South Plains SPCA office.

PELICAN: What does that mean?

ME: We have a lot of foster dogs, and they help us find homes for them.

PELICAN: What's a home?

ME: It's where we live. Where we eat and sleep and play.

PELICAN: Is this my home?

ME: It is for now. It's your foster home.

PELICAN: So, when we went to that SPCA place, was it different than our house? I can't remember.

ME: You didn't go in. Your sister Puffin and your brother Tanager went inside.

PELICAN: Are those the other puppies like me?

ME: They're kind of different from you. But yes.

PELICAN: How come I didn't go to the SPCA place?

ME: That's complicated. You and I went for a ride, instead.

PELICAN: When we saw the big water and the birds?

ME: Yes. You put your little nose up, sniffed the air, and then gave me a kiss.

PELICAN: I liked seeing the birds.

ME: Maybe you're a bird dog.

PELICAN: Mama? What's a bird dog?

ME: What do you think it might be?

PELICAN: Maybe I'm a dog and a bird.

ME: Perhaps so. You and your brothers and sisters are known as the Birdies.

PELICAN: Why??

ME: We like to have a group name for our foster dog families. You and your mama and siblings were all named for different birds.

PELICAN: A pelican is a bird?

ME: Yes.

PELICAN: Have I ever seen a pelican bird?

ME: No.

PELICAN: Why?

ME: Pelicans live by the ocean. Big, big water.

PELICAN: Bigger than the water you showed me?

ME: Much bigger. And farther away. We're landlocked here.

PELICAN: But I live here.

ME: Yes, you do.

PELICAN: This is difficult for such a small puppy to understand.

ME: You're a landlocked Pelican!

PELICAN: Oh, no!

ME: It's perfectly fine to be a landlocked Pelican. You're totally OK.

PELICAN: That's a relief!

PELICAN: What is a dog family?

ME: It's like all the dogs who came here with you. Your Mama Meadowlark and all your brothers and sisters.

PELICAN: All the puppies?

ME: Yes, all eight of you. And you had a daddy. His name is Rex Lee.

PELICAN: Is Rex Lee a bird?

ME: No, Rex Lee is a dog, a handsome red dog.

PELICAN: Is my Mama Meadowlark a bird?

ME: No, but she has a bird name. Meadowlarks are very pretty birds. And she might be partly bird dog.

PELICAN: So that's how I might be a bird dog?

ME: Yes.

PELICAN: So where did I come from?

ME: That's a complicated question. You came from Rex Lee and Meadowlark.

PELICAN: How?

ME: They each gave you some parts and those parts grew into you!

PELICAN: Where?

ME: Inside of your Mama Meadowlark.

PELICAN: What?!!

ME: Yep. You stayed in there for two months until you turned into a puppy.

PELICAN: This is very weird.

ME: Yeah, sounds made up, doesn't it?

PELICAN: You're telling me!

PELICAN: So how did I get out of Meadowlark, my mama?

ME: When you and your brothers and sisters grew into little puppies, then you came out.

PELICAN: We were ALL in there?!

ME: Yep.

PELICAN: Wow! It must have been really crowded!

ME: I would think so. You'll have to ask Mama Meadowlark about that sometime.

PELICAN: ALL of us? Are you sure?

ME: Yep. You were littler then.

PELICAN: That's a relief.

ME: Meadowlark probably thought so.

PELICAN: Did you see us puppies come out of Mama Meadowlark?

ME: I did not.

PELICAN: How do you know what happened?

ME: I've seen puppies come out of other mamas. The people who rescued you and your family thought you were a week old when they found you.

PELICAN: Where were we?

ME: In the woods. Living under a tree.

PELICAN: Oh, yeah. Was that a good place to be?

ME: Not really. It was dangerous because you puppies could have been eaten by coyotes or hawks.

PELICAN: Oh, no!!

ME: It's a good thing you were found and rescued!

PELICAN: Give that Tena person some more kisses, OK?

ME: OK.

8 puppies in the woods

Meadowlark

Rex Lee

PELICAN: We were under a tree? Were the trees like the sticks in the big dog yard?

ME: Like that, but bigger. Trees are the big green things. Sticks are pieces that fall off the trees.

PELICAN: Will all the sticks fall off?

ME: No, just a few.

PELICAN: Will I ever RUN OUT of sticks?!

ME: It seems not.

PELICAN: That's good.

PELICAN: I like the sticks in the big dog yard.

ME: You sure find a lot of them.

PELICAN: Sticks are good for Pelican.

ME: They are good to play with. Not so good to eat.

PELICAN: Why?

ME: A piece of a stick could get stuck inside you.

PELICAN: Is that the things puppies are made from inside our mamas? From sticks?

ME: Not exactly. Let's just say it's better to not eat the sticks.

PELICAN: I'll try to remember.

ME: Thank you.

PELICAN: Who knew there would be so many rules in life?

ME: More than you can imagine . . .

PELICAN: Where's my daddy?

ME: He's with a foster family in central Texas, near where you were all found.

PELICAN: Will he come here sometime?

ME: I don't think so. After he takes medicine for a few months and gets healthy, he'll find a family of people to live with.

PELICAN: Why does he need medicine?

ME: None of you were in good shape. Your mom and dad had worms in their intestines and in their hearts. You puppies all had skin infections.

PELICAN: That's terrible! Will we be OK?

ME: Yes, you're already doing much better. One of your brothers had to take medicine and the rest of you got well on your own.

ME: Your mom will need medicine for a few months for her heartworms.

PELICAN: Do I have worms?!

ME: Not in your heart, no.

PELICAN: That's good!

ME: It will take a couple of months for your mom to regain some weight, too. She was starved and trying to feed 8 puppies when she didn't have enough food herself!

PELICAN: She's my hero!

ME: She's a good one.

PELICAN: Make her better!

ME: I will do my best!

PELICAN: What is the box thing?

ME: It's a phone.

PELICAN: I like when it makes noises like dogs barking.

ME: I noticed you watching the dog videos.

PELICAN: Are there little tiny dogs inside the box?

ME: Sort of. It's mostly you and the other puppies.

PELICAN: Me?! I'm in the box?

ME: Yep.

PELICAN: Let me see me in the box, please.

ME: (shows the phone to Pelican)

PELICAN: I don't see anything.

ME: That's what you look like.

PELICAN: Like nothing?!

ME: Well, no. More like a puppy would look after trying to swim in his water bowl.

PELICAN: Is that a bad thing?

ME: (neutral face)

PELICAN: Where did we go, Mama?

ME: We went to the South Plains SPCA again to drop off Tanager and Puffin.

PELICAN: Was I supposed to go?

ME: (laughs) Well, some people think so.

PELICAN: Why they go there?

ME: Here's the thing. Every dog needs to find his or her people.

PELICAN: People?

ME: The tall animals like me who talk to you and love you, play with you, feed you, and make sure you have a bed. Every dog needs his or her own people.

PELICAN: So, Tanager and Puffin went there to meet their people?

ME: We hope so.

PELICAN: Then how come they go and I stay home?

ME: I'm trying to decide what's best for you. Should you go there and find new people or stay here with me and the big dogs?

PELICAN: (thinks hard)

ME: What do you think?

PELICAN: I'm thinking.

PELICAN: Why am I different from my brothers and sisters?

ME: What do you mean?

PELICAN: About going to the SPCA to find people.

ME: Sometimes your people are right in front of you, and you don't have to go anywhere to find them. If I'm your people, it would be wrong to take you there and let you go with other people. It's a hard thing to decide.

PELICAN: Why is it hard?

ME: There are lots of different kinds of people, and we want to find the best kind for you. Some homes have just one person, like here, and some have several people.

PELICAN: Is it better to have one people or lots of people?

ME: It can be good either way.

ME: Some homes have peoplepuppies, too. Little people. They are called children.

PELICAN: Would I like children?

ME: I feel sure you would.

PELICAN: I like big people, too!

ME: Some houses have other dogs—big dogs like we have here. Some have little dogs—and some have cats.

PELICAN: What are cats?

ME: Cats are animals. They are a bit like little dogs, but different.

PELICAN: This is complicated!

PELICAN: So, do I choose my people?

ME: You don't really have the experience to know the possibilities from which you would be choosing. You only know me and the people at the SPCA who give you your shots.

PELICAN: That's true. I'm still a little puppy.

ME: If you were choosing, what do you think you would choose?

PELICAN: I don't know! I like it here with you and the big dogs. But we don't have any peoplepuppies or cats, do we?

ME: Not right now. In the future, there will be peoplepuppies who will visit.

PELICAN: So, do you choose my people?

ME: I choose if your people are me or someone else.

PELICAN: OK. I love you. I'm going to go take a nap. Let me know when you decide.

ME: Good choice. I love you, too.

PELICAN: Mama, we haven't been talking much this week.

ME: Yeah, I've had things on my mind.

PELICAN: About me?

ME: Some of it. I've been thinking about what's best for you. But I didn't want to bother you, so I talked to my friends about it instead of talking to you.

PELICAN: OK.

ME: Now I think I need to have a talk with myself.

PELICAN: OK. I'll be over here with my stick if you need me.

ME: I imagined yesterday that you might become mine.

PELICAN: Am I?

ME: I think it would be good for you to stay here.

PELICAN: I like it here. I like you and the big dogs. And did you know we have little puppies?!!

ME: Yes. You were cute when you found the new foster puppies.

PELICAN: I said hello to them all.

ME: Yes, you did. You got in their pen and sniffed them very sweetly.

PELICAN: I like the puppies. Would they stay here also?

ME: No. Just you.

PELICAN: So, we wouldn't have puppies?

ME: Not all the time. But sometimes I help mamas and puppies who don't have anywhere to go.

PELICAN: So, we would have puppies sometimes.

ME: Yes.

PELICAN: I like the puppies.

ME: You went to the SPCA last night.

PELICAN: Umm-hmm.

ME: You seemed to enjoy the ride there.

PELICAN: I did! I liked the air-blowing thing.

ME: It ruffled up your fur in a very cute way.

PELICAN: I'm cute!

ME: Extremely cute.

PELICAN: Yay!

PELICAN: I was having fun with the air-blowing thing, but then that lady came and took me!

ME: Yes, Amber took you inside for your shots and your microchip.

PELICAN: The thing where they poked me?

ME: Yes.

PELICAN: I did NOT like that.

ME: What did you do?

PELICAN: I peed on them!

ME: (laughs) So I heard.

PELICAN: Was peeing on the lady not the right thing?

ME: It might have been better not to pee at that moment.

PELICAN: I was standing up for myself.

ME: I see. Are you sure you weren't just scared?

PELICAN: Oh. Maybe.

ME: It's OK. They poke you to give you stuff so you don't get sick.

PELICAN: I didn't know.

ME: Now you know.

PELICAN: Do I have to go there again?

ME: Yes, you'll need more shots.

PELICAN: I'll try not to pee on them next time.

ME: I appreciate that.

CHAPTER TWO
WHAT DOES JILL THINK?

ME: JILL, honey, how you doing?

JILL: I'm OK. Thanks, Mama!

ME: Not too stressed?

JILL: Well, I have a lot of jobs to do.

ME: And we have a lot of dogs around.

JILL: Yep. That makes me have more jobs.

ME: How so?

JILL: There are more dogs to protect.

ME: Do you sometimes protect them by growling or biting?

JILL: Yep.

ME: How does that work?

JILL: It's best for everyone if they do the right things. I help them know what the right things are.

ME: That makes sense. Thank you.

ME: What do you think of the puppy?

JILL: The little one with all the fur?

ME: Yes. I call him Pelican.

JILL: I like him. He's a nice puppy.

ME: Yes, he is.

JILL: We have a lot of puppies and extra dogs.

ME: Yes. I know that stresses you.

JILL: It's hard to be in charge of so many dogs and puppies.

ME: Well, it's my job to be in charge of them.

JILL: OK. It's good you're in charge. But there are things only the Big Dog can be in charge of.

ME: And that's you.

JILL: Of course.

ME: But this particular puppy. . . what if he didn't leave?

JILL: He would stay here like me and Marie and Gert?

ME: Exactly.

JILL: (thinks)

ME: So, did you think about the puppy?

JILL: Yes.

ME: Do you have questions for me?

JILL. Yes. If the puppy Pelican stays, am I in charge of him?

ME: Only for Big Dog stuff. I would be in charge of him for everything else.

JILL: So, I would growl or bite to show him what to do?

ME: Yes, in a Big Dog way . . . but not to hurt him.

JILL: Will he be this big forever? He's not very big.

ME: No, he'll get bigger. I'm not sure how big, but puppies get as big as their body tells them to get.

JILL: Oh.

ME: He might get as big as you. He probably will. He could be even bigger.

JILL: Oh!

ME: So, what have you been thinking about?

JILL: I've been thinking if the Pelican stays here and gets bigger than me, I probably should be nice to him now. Just in case.

ME: I think that is an excellent idea. Do you think you can do that?

JILL: I can try. I do like the Pelican.

ME: You've been pretty nice to him.

JILL: It was easier after those other puppies left.

ME: Yes, I could see that having Pelican, Puffin, *and* Tanager hanging out with the big dogs was stressful to you.

JILL: They were getting big! It was hard keeping them all doing the right things.

ME: I remember when Brodie was with us. Sometimes you were mean to him.

JILL: He wanted to be the Big Dog!!!

ME: He was the Big Boy Dog and you were the Big Girl Dog.

JILL: Uh-huh. (looks puzzled)

ME: But I think you wanted to be the Big Big Dog.

JILL: Yes!

ME: What if the puppy Pelican grows up wanting to be the Big Big Dog?

JILL: (thinks about it). I think that would be OK.

ME: Really?? (skeptical look)

JILL: I don't seem to care so much about being the Big Big Dog. Not like I used to.

ME: Maybe you're getting older and don't need such a responsible job.

JILL: Maybe so.

ME: But the part of you that wanted to be the Big Big Dog might sometimes get stirred up. I wouldn't want you to start fighting with Pelican the way you tried to fight with Brodie.

JILL: What do I do if that Big Big Dog part of me wakes up and wants to be the Big Big Dog again?

ME: I would suggest you think of me as the Big Big BIG Dog who doesn't want you to fight with your sisters and brother.

JILL: I will try to remember that.

ME: I will remind you if you need to be reminded. But I would rather you remember.

JILL: OK.

ME: I noticed you were playing very nicely with all the dogs this morning.

JILL: Yes. I usually just play with Marie, but today all the dogs needed me.

ME: You were even playing with Meadowlark.

JILL: Yes!

ME: She looked a little nervous.

JILL: I saw that.

ME: You played with Gert. And with the puppy Pelican.

JILL: I was on a roll!

ME: I was proud of you.

JILL: Yay!

JILL: Is Meadowlark staying too?

ME: No. She came here so I could help her take care of her puppies.

JILL: Is she done now?

ME: Yes. But she's stayed longer because she's sick.

JILL: She is? Is she going to drop dead like Brodie did?

ME: No. She has some worms in her heart that we are killing. After that she will find her people and go with them.

JILL: OK. I think that's for the best.

JILL: Mama, why were you crying this morning?

ME: I was thinking it might be best for Pelican to go to another family, like all our foster puppies do.

JILL: But Mama! He's OURS!

ME: (surprised) Really??

JILL: Yes ma'am. I thought you knew that.

ME: I keep changing my mind.

JILL: Change it back!

ME: You surprise me. I thought you would want things to stay like they are, just you and me and Gert and Marie.

JILL: Well, you and me and Gert and Marie are good. But the Pelican is kind of good too.

ME: He is, isn't he?

JILL: There's one problem, though. I don't think there's room on the bed for another dog.

ME: What do you think we might do about that?

JILL: Maybe that part of you and me and Marie and Gert should stay the same.

ME: Maybe the Pelican should sleep in his crate.

JILL: Yes!

ME: I notice that you 3 girls mostly take turns. You are on the bed before bedtime, but you always jump down when I turn off the lamp. Gert during the night. Marie for naps during the day.

JILL: True. It's one of my jobs to put you to bed. Are you saying the Pelican should have a turn too?

ME: We could think about it in the future. While he's still a young kid, we can hold off on giving him turns.

JILL: I like that plan.

ME: Here's something to think about. Since Pelican doesn't get a turn on the bed, he might sometimes sit in my lap instead.

JILL: I've noticed him in your lap, yes.

ME: It seemed to bother you.

JILL: It did at first, but then you explained to me that he's just a bitty puppy.

ME: Yes.

JILL: Did you notice this morning when you were holding the Pelican that I sat by your chair very nicely and wagged my tail?

ME: I did notice. I was proud of you. You let him have his turn and I was able to pet you also. I was pleased you didn't try to kill him for being closer me to at that moment than you were.

JILL: I'm a GOOD dog.

ME: Yes, you are. A bit territorial, but a good dog.

JILL: But of course.

CHAPTER THREE
WHAT DOES GERTRUDE STEIN THINK?

ME: I notice you've been playing with Pelican.

GERT: Is he that little hairy dog?

ME: Well, he's the puppy. We have another hairy dog, a preggo foster dog, but you haven't met her yet.

GERT: I like that puppy. Not all the time, though.

ME: At times, you guys play together really well.

GERT: Yes, but sometimes I just want to play with my toys.

ME: I can see that. What do you do at those times?

GERT: I play with my TOYS!

ME: And what if the puppy bothers you?

GERT: I bite his face.

ME: (laughing)

GERT: Why you laughing, Mama?

ME: I haven't seen you bite his face. You've never bitten any dog's face, to my knowledge.

GERT: Well, I *tell* him I'm gonna bite his face.

ME: And then what?

GERT: I play with my toy.

ME: And what happens if he tries to help you play?

GERT: I go around him.

ME: Now that I HAVE seen.

How to Adopt a Pelican

ME: What would you think about the Pelican staying here and living with us?

GERT: He already lives with us.

ME: Our foster puppies always move away, though.

GERT: Oh, yeah. True. So, this one wouldn't move away?

ME: I'm trying to decide. You're younger than the other two, and I thought he might be a good playmate for you.

GERT: I only play with you and with my green and purple rings.

ME: You do love the green and purple rings.

GERT: That puppy takes my toys sometimes!

PELICAN: I help you bring the toys back to Mama!

ME: You don't exactly bring them back, Mr. Pelican.

GERT: But I do!

ME: Yes, you do. It's very cute how you follow the Pelican and wait for your chance to steal your ring back.

GERT: Thanks, Mama. You're cute, too.

ME: Thank YOU!

ME: When the older dogs get old and pass on, would you want to have a dog friend still?

GERT: I don't understand this. Sorry, Mama.

ME: No worries. I'll let you know what I decide.

GERT: Would the Pelican sleep on the bed?

ME: Not for the foreseeable future. Since you three big girls have bed privileges. I don't think there's room for another dog.

GERT: It's important I sleep with you. As long as that doesn't change, I don't care if he lives here.

ME: Yours is less than a ringing endorsement, but I'll count it as your vote.

CHAPTER FOUR
WHAT DOES MARIE BRACQUEMOND THINK?

ME: What do you think of the puppy?

MARIE: I bite him.

ME: Why?

MARIE: He gets too close to me and puts his foot on my head!

ME: Yes. I see that.

MARIE: He bites my face, so I bite his face.

ME: I've also seen you be sweet with him.

MARIE: I was?

ME: Yes, you played with him, just a little bit.

MARIE: I forgot that.

ME: If Pelican stays here, do you think you can be his friend?

MARIE: Maybe . . .

ME: Do you bite his face because you don't like him?

MARIE: No . . .

ME: He seems to want you as his special friend.

MARIE: Oh!

ME: Do you bite his face because you're scared?

MARIE: Yes! What is he, exactly, anyway?

ME: He's a puppy. A little dog. He will grow up and be a big dog like the rest of you.

MARIE: Oh, OK. Well, that might be OK.

CHAPTER FIVE
WHAT DO I THINK?/SELF-THERAPY

ME: I decided this morning that Pelican should go for adoption.

OtherME: (cries for an hour)

ME: (cries for an hour)

OtherME: Why?

ME: I don't want to do all the stuff I would have to do.

OtherME: Like what?

ME: Brush him. Teach him to sit. Poop scoop. Figure out where he will sleep. It seems like too much to do.

OtherME: Those are things you know how to do.

ME: Yeah, I guess. I'm worried the other dogs might be unfriendly to him. I want him to have a buddy.

OtherME: Wouldn't you be his buddy?

ME: Yes, but I'd want him to have dog buddies, too. The other dogs are getting older though. Would a puppy be too much for them?

OtherME: Would they adjust?

ME: Probably . . .

OtherME: So, what's the problem?

ME: I want him to have dog friends. I see all those pictures of people's dogs where they sleep all cuddled together. I want that for Pelican.

OtherME: Do your dogs cuddle together?

ME: Not really. They touch sometimes when they all sleep on the bed, but I wouldn't call it cuddling. Maybe Marie and Gert, sometimes.

OtherME: Do they all cuddle with you?

ME: Yes.

OtherME: And does Pelican cuddle with you?

ME: Yes.

OtherME: And do other people's dogs always cuddle with one another?

ME: I don't know. Maybe.

OtherME: ---

ME: You mean the pics on social media aren't representative of what happens all the time?

OtherME: Mmm.

ME: What about travel?

OtherME: What about it?

ME: I've been running around all over the country for the last 4 years.

OtherME: For work or for fun?

ME: Both.

OtherME: When you traveled, didn't you have 4 dogs?

ME: At first. Then Brodie died. I missed him but it was much simpler to travel with 3. Especially since Jill tended to pick on Brodie. Even 3 was hard though.

OtherME: Are you going to travel again?

ME: I don't know.

OtherME: Will you be working in the future?

ME: I don't know! I don't think so. Maybe I'll write!

OtherME: You could still travel for fun . . . but without the land yacht?

ME: Yep. I gave it away.

OtherME: If you travel, how will you do it?

ME: I would drive somewhere. I'd still like to camp. Maybe with just one dog, in a tent.

OtherME: That sounds like fun, and simpler than the RV and 4 dogs. The other dogs would have a dog sitter?

ME: Yes, I think so.

OtherME: Would you fly places?

ME: Eventually.

OtherME: The dogs couldn't fly with you?

ME: No, they're too big. They would stay home with a dog sitter.

ME: I don't think you're understanding the 4-dog problem.

OtherME: Explain it to me.

ME: It's simple dog math.

OtherME: Math?

ME:
1 dog = 1 dog
2 dogs = 2 dogs
3 dogs = 7 dogs
4 dogs = 17 dogs

OtherME: I'll admit there's some truth in that.

ME: I've lived this truth. Trust me on this.

OtherME: Poop scooping.

ME: I hate it. I have a poop-scoop person who comes every other week, but with four big dogs, a lot of poop is in the yard in between her visits. Marie has already taught Pelican that poop is a tasty snack.

OtherME: Has Marie been harmed by this?

ME: Yes. It makes it hard to keep her weight down. She's always supplementing her diet with recycled dogfood, so to speak.

OtherME: Are there ways to solve this?

ME: None I'm very excited about.

OtherME: If Pelican gets adopted, would there be poop in the backyards at his new place?

ME: Probably. Or maybe he would get lucky and get adopted by a person who poop scoops every day.

OtherME: So?

ME: (sigh)

OtherME: Anything else?

ME: He eats sticks.

OtherME: And so?

ME: One of them might get stuck in his intestine. Maybe he should live with someone with a perfect lawn, someone that doesn't have sticks and bark everywhere.

OtherME: Is that likely?

ME: (mumbles) I don't know.

OtherME: (waits)

ME: I'm getting old.

OtherME: You're not that old.

ME: What if I die? It's an important question. What happens to my dogs?

OtherME: You can't take them with you. What happens to other people's dogs when they die?

ME: Different things. Sometimes they go with family or friends. Sometimes they are cruelly dropped off at a shelter.

OtherME: It's not a perfect world. Sometimes bad things happen.

ME: Yeah. But is it fair to adopt a young dog when I'm getting older?

OtherME: He's pretty charming. Don't you think someone would want him?

ME: Probably.

OtherME: Weren't your dogs adopted from the SPSPCA?

ME: Yeah. All three of them. Why?

OtherME: Don't they require that dogs be returned if a person can't take care of them?

ME: Well, yes.

OtherME: So, if friends or family can't take your dogs, they would go to the SPCA to find new homes?

ME: Well, yeah, but it would be stressful for volunteers to suddenly have to take in 3-4 medium to big dogs.

OtherME: But this is what they do? And most of their dogs arrive rather suddenly?

ME: Yeah.

OtherME: Maybe you could trust them to do that?

ME: Yeah. I hope so. I just hate to be a bother.

OtherME: You won't have to worry about it. You'll be dead.

ME: Pelican is very hairy.

OtherME: Don't you like hairy dogs the best?

ME: Sadly, yes.

OtherME: ---

ME: But . . . dog hair. Dog hair everywhere.

OtherME: Do you already have this problem?

ME: Sadly, yes. All the dogs are heavy shedders.

OtherME: What's one more, right?

ME: May I remind you about dog math?

OtherME: 4 dogs = 17 dogs?

ME: Yep.

ME: What if I trip over him?

OtherME: Does this happen a lot?

ME: I try to be careful.

OtherME: Have you fallen over a lot?

ME: No. A couple of times last year.

OtherME: What happened?

ME: I was trying to hurry through the front door without the dozen huge foster puppies on the patio getting ahead of me. I tripped on the doorsill.

OtherME: Any other time?

ME: Well, a couple of days ago.

OtherME: Did Pelican make you fall?

ME: Sort of. I was looking at him instead of watching where I was going.

OtherME: You fell? Were you hurt?

ME: A couple of goose eggs on my arm and knee.

OtherME: It wasn't exactly Pelican's fault.

ME: Just for being cute.

OtherME: You tripped because you got distracted?

ME: Yeah.

OtherME: ADHD much?

ME: Ya think?

OtherME: Have you asked the dogs if they mind Pelican joining the family?

ME: Yes.

OtherME: What did they say?

ME: They surprised me. They have some issues, but no deal-breakers.

OtherME: Even Jill?

ME: Especially Jill, as it turns out. She thinks he's ours.

OtherME: Well, is he?

ME: ---

OtherME: Anything else?

ME: Yeah. I don't want to listen to other people saying, "I knew it all along."

OtherME: Knew what?

ME: Knew I would keep him.

OtherME: Why?

ME: Because I never do. I let them all go. All the foster puppies I love. I never keep them, even if they're cute and I love them.

OtherME: Why would people say that?

ME: I've been very open about my thoughts about whether to adopt Pelican.

OtherME: Does it matter what people say?

ME: How old will I be when I learn this?

How to Adopt a Pelican

ME: I'm a person who doesn't keep my fosters.

OtherME: Have you had other dogs and puppies you loved and didn't want to give up?

ME: Yes.

OtherME: But you did give them up.

ME: Yes.

OtherME: But Pelican might be different?

ME: Maybe.

OtherME: Why is the Pelican different?

ME: It's hard to explain.

OtherME: Maybe now you will be a person who kept this one.

OtherME: Is anybody going to be mad about your decision?

ME: Maybe not mad, but disappointed.

OtherME: They will be disappointed if you give him up or if you keep him?

ME: Both. There are people I will disappoint either way. I've taught my friends to love him lately through Conversations with Pelican on social media and with photos of Pelican. They'll be disappointed if I give him up.

OtherME: Who else?

ME: There are the people at the SPCA. They would be disappointed because we try not to foster fail, i.e., keep our fosters.

OtherME: But the people at the SPCA have a goal of finding homes for dogs? They give a lot of time and effort to this?

ME: Yes. Just not our homes. (rueful laugh)

OtherME: Why do the SPCA people not want them to stay in your homes?

ME: We fear if fosters adopt too many dogs, they won't be able to foster anymore. Fosters are hard to find.

OtherME: And is that realistic?

ME: Yes.

OtherME: Might that happen with you?

ME: I don't think so.

OtherME: Why not?

ME: I treat my personal dogs and my foster dogs as two separate groups. Because . . . Jill.

OtherME: So?

ME: I don't think it would be a problem.

OtherME: You love Pelican.

ME: Yes.

OtherME: And he loves you?

ME: Yes, but he's a kid. He can learn to love anybody.

OtherME: He's an easy dog?

ME: So far.

OtherME: Do you think you should only take the complicated dogs?

ME: Maybe. That's how it's been. Jill, Marie, and Gert all had issues that made them unadoptable.

OtherME: Maybe it would be nice to have a dog that's not neurotic.

ME: It would be nice . . . but it's possible I might mess him up.

OtherME: Always possible.

ME: ---

How to Adopt a Pelican

ME: What if bad people were to adopt Pelican?

OtherME: Does that happen much?

ME: No.

OtherME: Are you in charge of that?

ME: No, why?

OtherME: (sigh) You're in charge of everything?

ME: Pretty much.

OtherME: In this house, you try to do the right things?

ME: Yep. Not perfectly, but I try.

OtherME: So . . . Pelican would probably have a good life with you. And if you croak, he would probably have a good life with someone else.

ME: I think so.

OtherME: Do you always have this much noise in your head?

ME: Yeah. Sorry.

CHAPTER SIX
WHAT DOES PELICAN THINK?

ME: Pelican, you seemed to have fun this morning.

PELICAN: It's all kind of a blur. What did I do?

ME: You went outside with all the mamas and then with the big dogs. You played with Autumn Moon's puppies. You played with Marie and Jill and Gert, and then you had breakfast.

PELICAN: Wow, that's a lot.

ME: There's more. You helped me gather up all the dog toys to go in the washer. You played outside with Mama Meadowlark. You ate some ice cubes.

PELICAN: I LOVE ice cubes. And all the mamas!!

ME: So I notice.

ME: After everything else you did, you went for a swim in the drinking water bowl and tried to jump in my lap.

PELICAN: I LOVE YOU!

ME: I love you, too, but you were dripping with cold water.

PELICAN: Sorry, Mama!

ME: I hollered and made you get off, so you went back out and rolled in the dirt.

PELICAN: I feel tired for some reason. I think I'll take a nap.

ME: You do that. A long one, maybe.

ME: Pelican, how would you like to stay here and live at the Tyler Dog Ranch?

PELICAN: Is that the name of this house?

ME: We call it that as a joke sometimes.

PELICAN: A dog ranch! Would I be a cowboy?!! OMG!

ME: You could be a cowboy. You'd be a cute one!

PELICAN: Or maybe I could be a cow dog?

ME: I don't think you would be a cow dog. You're basically a flop-eared fluffbutt.

PELICAN: A fluffbutt? That's a good thing to be, right?

ME: Yes. Fluffbutt is excellent.

PELICAN: I would live with you and the big dogs and the puppies and my mama?

ME: Well, mostly. Your mama will be getting her own place soon. You would be here with me and the big dogs. When we have foster mamas and puppies, you would live with them also.

PELICAN: That would be great! I'd be just like that girl in the picture box!

ME: (scratches head) What girl? Is this someone on TV?

PELICAN: Yes! She wanted to stay at a house with some people and they kept talking about it.

ME: Oh! You mean *Anne of Green Gables*?

PELICAN: Yes! She kept saying, "I hope you will let me stay," and they did! And then she had adventures!

ME: Now that's YOUR story. You're like *Annie of Green Gables!* You are the *Pelican of Toledo Avenue!*

PELICAN: I'm the PELICAN OF TOLEDO AVENUE!

ME: Welcome home!

PELICAN: Will my story ever be in the picture box?

ME: Anything's possible.

PELICAN: How would my story be in the box?

ME: Perhaps it could be in the smaller boxes. The phone and the computer. I could tell your story on social media.

PELICAN: I'd be famous! A famous fluffbutt! A famous cowboy! Woohoo! (runs in circles)

ME: You might want to know it's not always easy to be famous.

PELICAN: That's OK. Could we write a book?

ME: Honey, we're writing one now. All your stories are in it.

PELICAN: OMG! OMG! What's my book called?

ME: *HOW TO ADOPT A PELICAN.*

PELICAN: That's a good name! Adopting a Pelican is GOOD!

ME: It's VERY good.

PELICAN: I'll miss my Mama Meadowlark when she moves away. She bites my face and looks in my mouth and tells me what to do.

ME: It's a very weird thing the way she looks in your mouth every day.

PELICAN: She helps me!

ME: Yes. She's a good mama.

PELICAN: You said it!

CHAPTER SEVEN
THINGS I LOVE ABOUT PELICAN

The way he gets off the couch . . . one molecule at a time . . .

That he lets the puppies eat first . . .

How he makes it a point to play with everyone, even scary Jill . . .

That he calmly waits to see what's going on instead of milling around like the other dogs every time I make a move . . .

The way he thinks he's sleeping under the bed at naptime because his head is under the bed . . .

How much he loves ice cubes . . .

How fast he runs to his crate every night to wait for his bedtime snack . . .

How he helps me take a bath by staying nearby, licking water off my arm, plopping down on the bath mat to wait, etc. . . . .

How much he loves his toys . . .

His fluff . . .

CHAPTER EIGHT
THINGS I DO NOT LOVE ABOUT PELICAN

Instead of getting a big drink 2 or 3 times a day like a normal dog, he shoves his face in the water bowl for a sip many times daily. Next, he strings water several feet across the floor as it drips off his beard. And finally, he blots his wet icy cold beard on the back of my bare leg.

Every. Single. Time.

CHAPTER NINE
PUPPY DAZE

PELICAN: Mama, I like to sit on your lap.

ME: I like it when you do. I notice that you enjoy a cuddle now and then.

PELICAN: Yes, ma'am!

ME: You're very sweet with the earnest little kisses on my hand.

PELICAN: I love you.

ME: I love you too. I like it when you fall asleep and stay awhile.

PELICAN: Me, too!

PELICAN: Where do I go when I'm asleep?

ME: You're inside your own head, so your body can relax and recover.

PELICAN: Recover from what?

ME: From all the many things you do--and eat—when you're awake.

PELICAN: I'm inside my head? How do I fit inside my head?

ME: It's hard to explain.

PELICAN: I REALLY want to know!

ME: Umm. Dog magic.

PELICAN: Wow!

PELICAN: When I go in my crate, am I always there to sleep?

ME: Mostly. I notice you like to go in on your own for naps.

PELICAN: I LOVE my crate!

ME: You usually bark a few times when you go in at bedtime.

PELICAN: It's important for everyone to know where to find me.

ME: I would not have guessed that was the reason. I'll keep it in mind.

PELICAN: Thank you, Mama.

ME: Pelican, honey, you need to work on your housebreaking habits.

PELICAN: What do you mean?

ME: I mean you are supposed to pee outside.

PELICAN: Out in the backyard place?

ME: Yes.

PELICAN: I do! I pee on the patio, pee in the flowerbed over by the dying plant, pee in the backyard, and . . .

ME: Yes, you do. But sometimes you pee in the house.

PELICAN: I forget.

ME: When you're playing, you sometimes stop and pee suddenly.

PELICAN: I gotta go!

ME: You gotta go outside.

PELICAN: Even when I'm in a hurry?

ME: Even then. It only takes a few seconds to go to the back door.

PELICAN: OK. I'll try to remember.

ME: Oh, and about that peeing on the patio thing . . .

PELICAN: Am I not supposed to pee on the patio?

ME: I would prefer you go out into the yard and pee on the grass or dirt.

PELICAN: I'm in a hurry!

ME: It would be best to hurry on out into the yard then and not stop on the patio.

PELICAN: I'll try to remember.

ME: I'll remind you!

PELICAN: Thanks, Mama!

PELICAN: Mama, this is the best toy ever!

ME: I'm glad you like it. You are VERY enthusiastic.

PELICAN: I'm gonna play with it for hours and hours!

ME: So I see.

PELICAN: Does this toy have a name?

ME: Yes.

PELICAN: What's it called?

ME: The Lid to the Peanut Butter Jar.

PELICAN: That's a long name.

ME: Would you like to call it Lid?

PELICAN: Yes, ma'am!

ME: I noticed you barked at it.

PELICAN: I love my Lid.

PELICAN: I'm too tired to chew on the nice stick I brought in.

ME: Just as well, but what do you think is making you tired?

PELICAN: I think it's my new job, Mama.

ME: The job where you help take care of the foster puppies?

PELICAN: Yes!

ME: You've been working very hard at your job. Are you enjoying it?

PELICAN: Yes, ma'am!

ME: Your job has made you too tired to enjoy your sticks?

PELICAN: Yes, Mama. I'm going to have to take a nap instead.

ME: OK. It's good your job has flexible hours.

PELICAN: What does that mean?

ME: It means you can stop working and take a nap any time you wish.

PELICAN: That's an excellent job!

ME: We should all be so lucky.

ME: You are a sweet big brother, Pelican.

PELICAN: I LIKE the puppies.

ME: It appears you especially like Wentletrap.

PELICAN: Is he that busy little guy?

ME: Yes.

PELICAN: I keep an eye on him when I'm able.

ME: We all appreciate it, me and the other mamas.

PELICAN: Happy to do my job!

ME: I see you play mostly with the bigger foster puppies.

PELICAN: Yes, ma'am. I feel I know them better.

ME: Because you met them when they were still in the puppy box?

PELICAN: Yes. I liked playing with them in there.

ME: And they're bigger than the other puppies, even though they are younger.

PELICAN: I don't want to squash any of the little puppies.

ME: Well, thank you for being so careful.

PELICAN: My pleasure, ma'am.

ME: Pelican, you did not have a sterling day yesterday. Or this morning, so far.

PELICAN: (looks puzzled)

ME: You don't remember yesterday, do you?

PELICAN: With all due respect, ma'am, I'm a puppy.

ME: You certainly are.

PELICAN: So, did I do something bad?

ME: You chewed up my computer mouse, constantly brought in sticks and poop to eat, didn't come out of the puppy pen when I asked you to, and got your foot hung in the door to the pen. This morning you snarled and tried to bite me when I was holding you!

PELICAN: This does sound bad.

ME: You didn't seem to feel good this morning. I've never seen you snarl before. I wonder if you're in pain. Maybe your foot hurts or maybe you have a stomach full of twigs and computer parts? It's not like you to lash out.

PELICAN: Sorry, Mama!

ME: I noticed you didn't play with the puppies this morning. You just watched them through the glass door.

PELICAN: I'm so sorry. I don't remember. I feel OK now.

ME: I truly hope your stomach is not full of sticks and computer parts. That's why we stayed in today. We're having afternoon quiet time so I can watch a movie in peace. Thank you for going into your crate so nicely.

PELICAN: Thank you for the toys in my crate.

ME: No problem.

ME: Pelican, Pelican!

PELICAN: I'm a mess, Mama.

ME: Yep. You are a huge mess. You are covered in poop from head to tail.

PELICAN: I had an accident.

ME: You pooped AND threw up in your crate overnight.

PELICAN I'm not sure what happened.

ME: When we go outside at bedtime in the future, it might help for you to pay more attention to pooping and less attention to sticks.

PELICAN: I'll try to remember, Mama.

ME: Thank you!

How to Adopt a Pelican

PELICAN: What was that?!!

ME: It was your first bath.

PELICAN: I thought I was going to die!

ME: You surprised me, since you seem to love to play in the water.

PELICAN: That was water?!

ME: Yes, sir. Just like in the water bowl you stick your whole face into multiple times every day and the puppy swimming pool in which you played with your siblings.

PELICAN: I did not think it was water!

ME: You had to have a bath to get all the poop off of you.

PELICAN: Maybe next time we could wait for it to fall off.

ME: That probably won't happen.

PELICAN: I smell different after my bath.

ME: Soap and water can have that effect.

PELICAN: I'm very clean now.

ME: I would love to think you would stay clean for a while.

PELICAN: That would be good!

ME: I'm not optimistic.

PELICAN: Me, neither.

How to Adopt a Pelican

ME: You've been very busy with your new job.

PELICAN: I worked hard yesterday!

ME: Yes, you did! It's nice that you've taken some time this morning for a nap and a cuddle.

PELICAN: It's nice to visit you. It's like being a puppy again!

ME: You will be 4 months old tomorrow!

PELICAN: Is that very old?

ME: Nope. You're still practically brand-new.

PELICAN: That's good!

ME: You have no idea.

ME: Mr. Pelican, you seem to have had a good day so far.

PELICAN: Yes, ma'am!

ME: You played with all the dogs, had breakfast with the puppies, played with your toys, and now you're having a wrestling match with your mama and Autumn Moon.

PELICAN: Ain't it great?!

ME: It's pretty great, yeah.

PELICAN: (kisses)

ME: I noticed you started with one ear kaboom and progressed to double kabooms.

PELICAN: Mama, why do my ears kaboom?

ME: I have no idea.

PELICAN: Does it hurt my ears to have them go kaboom?

ME: It doesn't appear to. They're just flipping inside out. It seems harmless enough, but it does make you very cute.

PELICAN: Thank you, Mama!

ME: Thank YOU!

PELICAN: For what?

ME: For making me laugh.

PELICAN: Aw.

ME: Pelican, I notice you're not much for chasing things.

PELICAN: Chasing things, Mama?

ME: Yes. For instance, if I throw a toy over there, you don't seem inclined to go get it.

PELICAN: I assume if you threw it over there, that's where you wanted it.

ME: I guess that explains your point of view, anyway.

PELICAN: Thanks.

ME: Some dogs like to play by chasing things people throw. They run after them and bring the items back to be thrown again.

PELICAN: Interesting . . .

How to Adopt a Pelican

PELICAN: Mama, what was that we did?!

ME: We went for a drive. Just you and me.

PELICAN: You took my picture!

ME: That's kind of a given.

PELICAN: And then we stopped at the park place to look at the birds!

ME: Yep. After a bit we got out and walked around.

PELICAN: I didn't know the park was for walking on!

ME: You finished your puppy shots recently, so now you can go more places.

PELICAN: I'm getting all grown up.

ME: (sniff)

ME: Our trip to the park was your second time to wear a collar and your first time to have a leash.

PELICAN: Was that the string thing?

ME: Yes. You did pretty well. Of course, my idea was to follow you where you went so that the leash wasn't a big deal.

PELICAN: There was p-mail waiting for me at the park!

ME: Your first p-mails!

PELICAN: I like checking my p-mail.

ME: Maybe sometime you can send some p-mail to another dog.

PELICAN: This growing-up thing is pretty good stuff.

How to Adopt a Pelican

ME: Pelican, could you get any cuter?

PELICAN: I don't know, Mama. I could try.

ME: I see you're sleeping with the stuffed turtle.

PELICAN: He's my favorite turtle.

ME: The turtle has been a good friend to many puppies.

PELICAN: Now he's my good friend!

ME: I enjoy our playtime after breakfast.

PELICAN: Me, too!

ME: I've had to remind you the last couple of days not to bite.

PELICAN: I'm sorry. I forget.

ME: Remembering not to bite people is an important thing.

PELICAN: I can bite my toy?

ME: Yes. That's part of why you have toys.

PELICAN: I love my rope toy.

ME: Your toy du jour.

PELICAN: What's a du jour?

ME: It means a special thing you like or have today, but it probably won't be your favorite thing tomorrow.

PELICAN: Yes! I'm du jouring the heck out of my rope toy.

ME: I'm glad you like your toy. It definitely beats bringing in a piece of desiccated poop for playtime.

PELICAN: I like poop, too!

ME: Yes, you do.

PELICAN: Sometimes I du jour the heck out of that poop.

ME: So you do.
.

ME: I see the rope toy, yesterday's toy du jour, has been replaced by the little blue bone.

PELICAN: I'm keeping my rope toy handy just in case I need to du jour it. And my turtle.

ME: I notice lately you've developed a new take on the ear kaboom.

PELICAN: What did I take?

ME: You didn't take anything. You have an ear flop. I've never seen a dog who can flop his ear over to the middle of his forehead.

PELICAN: My ears have a life of their own, Mama.

ME: So it seems.

How to Adopt a Pelican

PELICAN: That was fun!!

ME: Pelican, Pelican!

PELICAN: You know, the thing where we got in the box thing and went someplace!

ME: The box thing is called the truck.

PELICAN: Yes!

ME: Ok. Let's review. You went in the backyard so you could take care of your business before we left, then we got in the truck, drove maybe a mile or mile-and-a-half. You peed on the front floorboard and then sat in the truck while I bought gas.

PELICAN: I didn't know if you were coming back!

ME: I was literally 3 feet away at the gas pump and clearly visible through the window. And then I got back in and drove 2 or 3 miles to Target for our curbside pickup. While the lady got our stuff, you pooped on the back floorboard.

PELICAN: I HAD to go.

ME: Next time go in the backyard, please.

PELICAN: I'll try to remember.

ME: We then drove about 3 or 4 miles with the windows down because of the poop stench and stopped at the post office to mail some letters in the outside box. When we headed home, you started throwing up in the front seat.

PELICAN: I'm sorry. I didn't feel right.

ME: We're going to have to figure out a way to help with your carsickness. I hoped a few short trips would get you used to being in the truck, but you throw up every time.

PELICAN: Not every time!

ME: True that. You didn't throw up Monday night when we took you and the Moon puppies and Autumn Moon to the SPCA. Maybe you need a dog friend along.

PELICAN: If I do throw up, my dog friend could help me clean it up.

ME: Yuck.

How to Adopt a Pelican

PELICAN: Mama, why I haz no job?

ME: You are presently on vacation.

PELICAN: What does that mean?

ME: It means you still have a job, but you don't need to do it today.

PELICAN: OK, but I like my job.

ME: Today your job is to consider your work/life balance.

PELICAN: What does that mean?

ME: It means we pretend in our culture we can strike a balance between work and other parts of our lives. We do this partly by taking vacations.

PELICAN: This is hard for a puppy to understand.

ME: I know. It's a hard idea for people, too.

PELICAN: Where are my puppies?

ME: They went to the SPCA to find their people.

PELICAN: Oh! That's why I'm on vacation?

ME: Yes, sir.

ME: Pelican, your Mama Meadowlark is going to move to a different house soon.

PELICAN: She won't live here anymore?!

ME: No. She will be adopted.

PELICAN: Will I still live here?

ME: Yes. You're staying. You're the Pelican of Toledo Avenue, remember?

PELICAN: Yay! But I'll miss my mama.

ME: I know. Sorry.

PELICAN: Who's going to play with me after Mama Meadowlark moves away?

ME: That's a good question. I hope you and Gertrude Stein play together. She's the youngest of your new sisters.

PELICAN: I like to play with Marie.

ME: The one who growls when you put your foot on her head?

PELICAN: Yes! She doesn't mean anything bad by it. She loves me.

ME: Sometimes we'll have puppies for you to enjoy and help raise.

PELICAN: That's good! I LOVE puppies.

ME: I doubt any of the other dogs will wash your face for you like your mama does.

PELICAN: How will I be clean?

ME: I guess that will be for you to figure out. I hope you don't blot your cold, wet beard on the back of my leg all the time.

PELICAN: I'll try to remember.

ME: Oh, I saw you checking out your mom's boobs this morning. She hasn't had milk for three months.

PELICAN: I like to check every now and then, just in case it comes back.

ME: Pelican, Pelican.

How to Adopt a Pelican

PELICAN: Mama, I haven't seen these toys before.

ME: They're new.

PELICAN: Are they for me?!

ME: Yes, sir. For you and your dog friends.

PELICAN: Are the toys to replace those body parts the dog doctor took away?

ME: Oh! (laughs nervously) No, not necessarily.

PELICAN: I wondered.

ME: It's more in hopes that if you have enough toys to play with, the *NEW* TV remote and the *NEW* computer mouse will be safer.

PELICAN: I like this toy that looks like a stick.

ME: Good! It's like a stick, but healthier for you than an actual stick.

PELICAN: Thank you for the new toys!

ME: My pleasure.

PELICAN: Does that mean you're going to play with the toys also?

ME: No, it means it gives me pleasure to provide you with toys, especially if they work as advertised.

ME: Pelican, you're a blur.

PELICAN: SO much fun!

ME: Helping Mama take a bath?

PELICAN: Yes, ma'am!

ME: It seemed surprisingly interesting to you.

PELICAN: I love the water!

ME: I thought at one point you might jump in.

PELICAN: I thought about it. Water is SO great!

ME: You seem to be channeling your late Uncle Brodie. He loved to come in and help with bath time.

PELICAN: Why's he late?

ME: That means he's no longer with us.

PELICAN: So, is helping with bath time another of my jobs?

ME: Would you like it to be?

PELICAN: Yes, ma'am!

ME: You came out of it with a really cute hairdo.

PELICAN: What does that mean?

ME: It means when you were helping with the bath, I petted you with a wet hand and made the hair on top of your head stand up. You look very stylish.

PELICAN: Thank you, ma'am! So do you.

ME: (wrapped in bath towel) Umm, thank you.

ME: Pelican, you look a little tired for a puppy who just slept 10 hours.

PELICAN: It wasn't just sleep. I went into the backyard place and played with the big dogs.

ME: For like an hour, if that. 30 minutes, maybe.

PELICAN: Perhaps it was breakfast that made me tired.

ME: Well, you go ahead and lounge around. I'm sure you'll perk up later.

PELICAN: Yes, ma'am!

ME: You're sleeping on top of Mama Meadowlark.

PELICAN: Yes ma'am! She doesn't mind.

ME: How do we know this?

PELICAN: She would tell me.

ME: I remember last week you were sleeping on Gert. She seemed to mind.

PELICAN: (puzzled) My dog friends love me!

ME: Well, you definitely motor ahead as if that's true.

PELICAN: Mama?

ME: They love you.

ME: I notice your mom is doing your daily dental.

PELICAN: I said no!! No, No to Mama Meadowlark! I didn't open my mouth for her today.

ME: So I see.

PELICAN: She licks my throat!

ME: I understand why you would say no.

PELICAN: It just ain't right, Mama.

ME: It IS a little weird.

PELICAN: You said it!

ME: Pelican, you make me laugh.

PELICAN: What did I do, Mama?

ME: Well, first you only got half of yourself off the sofa when you wanted to eat a random piece of debris off the rug.

PELICAN: No point doing the extra work of getting the other half of me down.

ME: I see. And then later you just sat on the floor while everyone was milling about.

PELICAN: I didn't know what we were doing.

ME: Neither did they, but every time I stand up, close my laptop computer, or even just uncross my ankles, everyone starts milling around.

PELICAN: It seemed to be a good idea to wait and see.

ME: I can't tell you how happy I am to hear that.

PELICAN: What was that?!

ME: These are called scissors.

PELICAN: What happened?

ME: Well, nothing terrible.

PELICAN: I kind of fuzzed out.

ME: Yeah, that's exactly the problem. You have this fuzzy hair that grows toward the middle of your face and gets in front of your eyeballs. I used the scissors to trim it.

PELICAN: Why?

ME: So that you don't have to look through at the world through a haze of fuzzy hair.

PELICAN: I don't mind.

ME: We wouldn't want that hair to poke you in the eye.

PELICAN: I wouldn't like that.

ME: There you go.

PELICAN: OK, thanks Mama.

ME: I will say I've never seen a dog your size turn into such a tiny little ball. You rolled up so small you were almost invisible!

PELICAN: I'm a flea! Ha ha ha!

ME: You're a very cute little flea now that your eyeball hair has been trimmed.

PELICAN: Thanks, Mama!

Pelican and siblings

Cheryl M Tyler is a full-time writer living in Texas with her family of dogs. She writes humorous stories about her dogs Pelican and Bennie. She's also the author of a series of novels entitled Complicated Lives.

She is a retired physician and has fostered over 200 dogs in the past 20 years. She has a special interest in pregnant and nursing moms and puppies, including orphaned pups.

She knows for a fact some dogs can talk and they have a great deal to say about life if only we listen.

Read all the Conversations with Pelican!

How to Adopt a Pelican
Sorry, Mama!
The Perplexed Pelican
Pelican of Toledo Avenue
Fluffbutt Cowboy

Check out the Conversations with Bennie series!

Life of Bennie
Bennie and the Pets
I Get by with Help from My People
The Hair Snatchers!
Gentleman Dog about Town
Home Sweet Doghouse

*****

**If you're up for a more serious read, take a look at these novels by author Cheryl M Tyler.
They are emotional stories of physicians juggling complex personal and professional lives.**

Star Mountain
Luckenbach North
Two-Part Inventions
Visiting Hollister

(Some titles pending publication.)

Made in the USA
Coppell, TX
23 September 2021